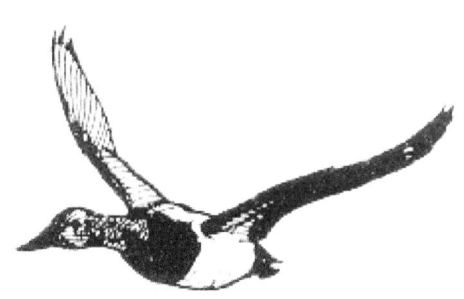

The North American Bird Conservation Initiative in the United States:

A Vision of American Bird Conservation

U.S. NABCI Committee
September 2000

THE NORTH AMERICAN BIRD CONSERVATION INITIATIVE IN THE UNITED STATES:
A Vision of American Bird Conservation

EXECUTIVE SUMMARY

Birds have always been a source of inspiration and fascination to people around the globe and from all walks of life. In the United States, nature-based recreation—from backyard feeders to regional festivals—is the fastest growing segment of the tourism industry. In 1996, approximately 160 million Americans, or 77% of the population, spent $29.2 billion to observe, photograph, or feed wildlife—an increase of more than 39% since 1991. If wildlife watching were a corporation, it would have ranked 23rd on the *Fortune 500* list that year. A high percentage of this recreation involves birds. Birding is growing faster than many other outdoor recreational activities such as biking, pleasure walking, skiing, and golfing; it increased 200% from 21 million participants in 1982-83 to an estimated 63 million in 1997. Birders spend some $20 billion annually in seed, travel, and equipment. The number of major birding festivals has grown from five in 1985 to 140 in 1999. At a National level, economic activity directly associated with enjoyment of birds generated over 191,000 jobs and more than $895 million in sales and income tax revenues in 1991. In addition, three million migratory bird hunters generated $1.3 billion in retail sales, having a total economic multiplier effect of $3.9 billion—considering the 46,000 additional jobs and $176 million in sales and income tax revenues produced.

America's bird population, however, is showing an alarming decline. Long-term radar records reveal that numbers of migratory birds passing over the Louisiana Gulf Coast have declined by half since the 1960s. Birds such as the cerulean warbler, king rail, loggerhead shrike, and painted bunting have exhibited a striking decline of 60-75%. The ruffed grouse, eastern meadowlark, northern bobwhite, and American bittern have lost 50-58% of their populations, while even more well-known birds such as the robin, goldfinch, and whip-poor-will have declined by about 20% in recent years. In greatest jeopardy are the 85 bird species currently on the U.S. Fish and Wildlife Service's threatened and endangered species list.

Many federal, state, and non-governmental wildlife agencies and organizations working in the United States and abroad have noted the development of this alarming trend. To address the needs of various bird groups, they have joined forces in several extensive partnerships. Some of these individual initiatives include:

- North American Waterfowl Management Plan
- Partners in Flight
- U.S. Shorebird Conservation Plan
- North American Colonial Waterbird Conservation Plan

While these efforts have generated some successes, it has been increasingly recognized that the overlapping conservation interests of these initiatives could be better served through more integrated planning and delivery of bird conservation. The **North American Bird Conservation Initiative in the United States** (NABCI-US) arose out of this realization.

The vision of NABCI-US is simply to see:

> *Populations and habitats of North America's birds protected, restored, and enhanced through coordinated efforts at international, national, regional, state, and local levels, guided by sound science and effective management.*

The NABCI-US seeks to accomplish this vision by (1) broadening bird conservation partnerships; (2) working to increase the financial resources available for conserving birds in the United States and wherever else they may occur throughout their life cycle; and (3) enhancing the effectiveness of those resources and partnerships by facilitating integrated bird conservation.

The NABCI-US will be guided by a set of principles that establish an operational framework within which this initiative and its partners may conduct integrated bird conservation in the United States and in other countries where these birds spend portions of their life cycles. These principles will articulate a common understanding of the relationship between NABCI-US, individual bird conservation initiatives, and partners. Such understanding will insure recognition of federal legislative and international treaty obligations and state authorities, and foster respect for the identity and autonomy of each initiative. A brief history and status of the major North American bird conservation initiatives is included. The fundamental components of the conservation approach to be used by NABCI-US are expressed within its goal:

> *To deliver the full spectrum of bird conservation through regionally based, biologically driven, landscape-oriented partnerships.*

In striving to accomplish this goal, NABCI-US partners are working together "to take bird conservation to the next level."

Birds have a unique relationship with humans because they share our lives in ways that other groups of wildlife species do not. Because of their unique status in human societies, the protection and restoration of bird populations and habitats demands and deserves special emphasis among our conservation efforts. Fortunately, these efforts will directly benefit the environment and habitats shared by virtually all other species—including ours.

TABLE OF CONTENTS

ACKNOWLEDGEMENTS

The U.S. NABCI Committee gratefully acknowledges the efforts of the Interim U.S. NABCI Steering Committee in drafting this document. Committee members devoted considerable energies to accomplishing the task of developing this vision, working through many edifying discussions, debates, and email exchanges to reach a consensus draft vision. The members of that Committee were:

Scott C. Yaich, Chair
Arkansas Game and Fish Commission

Jon Andrew
U.S. Fish and Wildlife Service, Division of Migratory Bird Management

Ken Babcock
Ducks Unlimited

Vernon Bevill
Texas Parks and Wildlife Department

Stephen Brown
Manomet Center for Conservation Sciences

James Kushlan
U.S. Geological Survey, Biological Research Division

Tony Melchiors
Weyerhaeuser Company

Gary Myers
Tennessee Wildlife Resources Agency

David Pashley
American Bird Conservancy

David Smith
U.S. Fish and Wildlife Service, Division of North American Waterfowl and Wetlands

Melanie Steinkamp
U.S. Geological Survey, Biological Research Division

In turn the Interim Committee members are grateful for having been provided the opportunity to contribute to this effort. We acknowledge the efforts of the many individuals who provided comments and suggestions that contributed to the constructive revision of this document. Their efforts helped forge a vision that we hope will help provide focus to the direction of bird conservation in the United States and beyond during these early years of the 21st century.

THE NORTH AMERICAN BIRD CONSERVATION INITIATIVE IN THE UNITED STATES:
A Vision of American Bird Conservation

INTRODUCTION

Birds. Their capacity for flight has always captured our imagination and been the envy of earth-bound humans. It also accounts for their widespread distribution; a cha shared by humans that further strengthens our truly unique relationship with b do we thrill to the sight of the first robin of the spring, a pair of wild turkeys, solitary bald eagle gliding across a lake? How many of us have paused while raking leaves in the fall to reflect on the wonders of migration as we watched and listened to a flock of geese overhead traveling south? How many times have we camped in the woods with our families, perhaps beside a lake, and listened thoughtfully as whip-poor-wills or owls called in the darkness? How many sunbathers have peacefully watched pelicans skim surf, or smiled at shorebirds racing up and down the beach at the edge of the How many of us have been struck by the fragility of life and felt sadness in fi lifeless form of a small bird which failed to comprehend "window"?

We as individuals and as a society have a unique relationship with birds, which touch us in ways that other wildlife species do not. Because of their special status in our society and their unique behaviors and habits, there is a growing sense of urgency among us to ensure their conservation. Fortunately, this status provides an opportunity for bird conservation to serve as an "umbrella" for the conservation of other wildlife species, biological diversity, and natural resources. Thus, *the vision of protecting and restoring the populations and habitats of North America's birds* demands and deserves special emphasis among conservation efforts—and the time is *now*.

PURPOSE, VISION, AND GOAL

- *Purpose*

In 1962, four years before the initiation of the Breeding Bird Survey, Rachel Carson elevated the issue of declining bird populations within the national consciousness through her book *Silent Spring*. She was among the first to sound the alarm on behalf of bird conservation in a way that resonated with the public. Carson dedicated her book to Dr. Albert Schweitzer, citing his quote:

> *"Man has lost the capacity to foresee and to forestall.*
> *He will end by destroying the earth."*

Fortunately, attitudes toward conservation have progressed since 1962 and we now have more reason for cautious optimism. We have begun to *foresee* solutions to the problems confronting bird conservation, although the broad-based commitment necessary to reverse the declines has yet to be fully made. We have even begun to *forestall* some of the problems, but on a limited basis and for a minority of bird species.

Bird conservation stands at the edge of a major advancement. This document portrays a vision for the future of bird conservation in the United States, and lays out a fundamental process that can "take bird conservation to the next level" across North America and beyond. In so doing, its primary purposes are to help:

> *(1) initiate and broaden bird conservation partnerships;*
> *(2) increase financial resources available for conserving birds in the United States and wherever else they may occur during their life cycles; and,*
> *(3) enhance the effectiveness of those resources and partnerships by facilitating integrated bird conservation.*

- **Vision**

The vision of the North American Bird Conservation Initiative in the United States (NABCI-US), for the enjoyment of current and future generations, is to see:

> *Populations and habitats of North America's birds protected, restored, or enhanced through coordinated efforts at international, national, regional, state, and local levels, guided by sound science and effective management.*

The focus of this document is a bird conservation vision for the United States. However, most bird species in the United States are migratory and many have a continental, even hemispheric, geographic distribution. For U.S. efforts to be successful, they must also address the needs of these birds while outside the United States. Thus, U.S. efforts must include a strong international component. Integrated delivery of the U.S. initiative with and through the broader North American Bird Conservation Initiative (NABCI), along with actions beyond our continental borders, are necessary for the successful realization of this vision.

- **Goal**

The goal of the NABCI-US is:

> *To deliver the full spectrum of bird conservation through regionally based, biologically driven, landscape-oriented partnerships.*

ECONOMIC VALUE OF BIRDS

Birds not only inspire our poets and our spirits, but also provide the basis for a significant and rapidly growing economy. Our level of participation in bird-related recreation is a strong indicator of their value to society. Nature-based recreation is the fastest growing segment of the tourism industry, increasing approximately 30% annually since 1987. Seventy-seven percent of U.S. citizens, or 160 million, spent $29.2 billion in 1996 to observe, photograph, or feed wildlife—39% more dollars than 1991. If wildlife watching were a corporation, it would have ranked 23rd on the *Fortune 500* list that year.

A high proportion of nature-based tourism includes birds. Birding is growing faster than many other outdoor recreational activities such as biking, pleasure walking, skiing, and golfing. It increased 200% from 21 million participants in 1982-83 to an estimated 63 million in 1997. Collectively, birders spend approximately $20 billion per year on backyard bird-feeding, travel, and paraphernalia. An active group, 24.7 million birders took trips away from home in 1991 to participate in birding activities, spending $5.2 billion on goods and services.

The number of significant birding festivals across the Nation soared from five in 1985 to 140 in 1999. The Texas Rio Grande Birding Festival generated $266,000 for the local economy in 1994; this exploded to $1.6 million only two years later. In fact, revenue from birding-related tourism in the Lower Rio Grande Valley of Texas now exceeds that from the area's citrus industry. Similarly, the Delaware Bay shore and Cape May peninsula of New Jersey receive more than $40 million annually from birders alone. At a National level, economic activity directly associated with the non-consumptive enjoyment of birds generated 191,000 jobs and more than $895 million in sales and income tax revenues in 1991. In addition, three million migratory bird hunters generated $1.3 billion in retail sales, having a total economic multiplier effect of $3.9 billion—considering the 46,000 additional jobs and $176 million in sales and income tax revenues produced.

These examples illustrate the actual and potential economic *benefits* of birds and their conservation. However, there are also important economic *costs of failing* to conserve birds. There are approximately 85 bird species on the U.S. Fish and Wildlife Service's threatened and endangered species list. If bird populations decline to the level of being threatened or endangered, costs for their conservation escalate dramatically. For example, in 1995, $18.5 million was spent on the conservation and recovery of the northern spotted owl, while $15.7 million was spent on the marbled murrelet, $8.3 million on the red-cockaded woodpecker, and $6.4 million on the bald eagle.

Birds are integral parts of our landscapes, performing important, sometimes irreplaceable functions carrying tremendous costs to society should they be lost or diminished. Birds pollinate plants, disperse seeds, are critical links in the food web, and play significant roles in insect pest control. Insects and pathogens cause greater forest losses than any other agent, including fire. One study documented that insect-eating forest birds reduced the number of insects on white oak saplings by half, enhancing tree growth and resulting in approximately 17% greater biomass production. With a projected loss of 28 million acres of forest land and an estimated 40% increase in wood consumption by 2040, the Nation can ill-afford additional losses in productivity due to declining populations of insect-eating forest birds in our remaining forest lands.

URGENCY AND NEED

Over 700 bird species occur in the United States. Populations of many once-common birds are gradually shifting toward scarcity while other species, such as the double-crested cormorant, lesser snow goose, and giant Canada goose, have adapted perhaps too well to our altered environment. Addressing both scarcity and overabundance is a significant challenge for bird conservation today.

One expression of the current vision of bird conservation is "to keep common birds common." Perhaps the most startling concern involves well-known species that are slipping gradually out of the ranks of the common and into those of the rare. Cerulean warblers have declined an average of 4.2% per year, or an alarming 75% overall since 1966. Similarly striking declines of 60-70% have been documented for the olive-sided flycatcher, king rail, loggerhead shrike, painted bunting, and black tern; and 50-58% declines for the ruffed grouse, eastern meadowlark, northern bobwhite, and American bittern. Even some of the most common birds are becoming less so. For example, how many people realize that American goldfinch and whip-poor-will populations have declined by approximately 20% since 1966?

Unfortunately, these examples are not unique or isolated. Long-term radar records show that in the late 1980's only half as many waves of migratory birds passed over the Louisiana Gulf Coast than in the 1960's. Among those species highly associated with grasslands, population indices for only two have increased since 1966, whereas 23 have decreased. Over the last quarter century, 18 of the 24 species of shorebirds for which data are available have also shown notable declines.

Birds that migrate to the Neotropics in the winter comprise up to 80% of the species nesting in eastern deciduous forests. Eighty percent of these are the insectivores so important to forest health and productivity. From 1978 to 1987, 45% of these species declined significantly. Over the last 30 years, 8 of the 19 forest-breeding species in the Blue Ridge Mountains and 13 of the 44 in the Adirondacks have also declined. Of the 417 species monitored by the Breeding Bird Survey since 1966, approximately 50% exhibit long-term declining trends.

The urgency to address bird conservation can be highlighted using the example of the piping plover, listed as endangered in 1985. If the current decline of 7% per year continues, the piping plover will be extinct in about 80 years. The Great Plains population objective is 2,550 pairs. If management actions could reverse the declining population trend and foster an annual 1% increase beginning today, the species would reach its target population for de-listing in 53 years. However, a delay of only 1 year in reversing that declining population trend delays reaching the recovery level by 13 years; and a delay of 5 years postpones attainment of the objective by 63 years. Thus, the biological realities of the dramatic, long-term declines of many bird populations, coupled with the societal and economic incentives for their conservation, illustrate the urgency facing bird conservation.

One of the best-known bird-based metaphors is "a canary in a coal mine." It was once a common practice for miners to take canaries into mines with them to serve as "living alarms" for environmental danger. Being more sensitive than humans to poisonous gases in the mines, dying canaries warned miners to get out before they too were overcome. In the simple ecosystem of a coal mine composed only of rock, air, miners, and canaries, an environmental challenge such as poisonous gas can rapidly and noticeably upset the entire ecosystem. Today, many believe that birds in our natural ecosystems are serving as present-day canaries in the coal mine. Although the complexities and subtleties of natural ecosystems generally preclude anything as sudden and dramatic as a dead canary in a cage, declines in many of our bird populations may be warning us of environmental challenges that also bear danger for our society and quality of life if not addressed.

OPPORTUNITY

Tremendous potential exists to improve bird conservation, including all aspects of protection, restoration, and enhancement in the United States and abroad. Currently there is a growing level of public interest in and support for birds. We are also experiencing an unprecedented period of economic prosperity. There are many strong existing partnerships to build upon, as well as new ones being formed, for planning and implementing bird conservation. Fortunately, we have excellent models from which to learn.

Restoration of the bald eagle and peregrine falcon involved highly successful bird conservation efforts using the single-species approach. Cooperative management actions between Federal and state agencies and private conservation organizations resulted in the removal of both species from the Federal list of endangered species.

Applying a more integrated ecosystem approach, the North American Waterfowl Management Plan (NAWMP) is pre-eminent among successful bird conservation models. Since 1986, its implementation has helped increase many waterfowl populations. Most importantly, it institutionalized partnerships as the *best* avenue to successful wildlife resource conservation. State and federal agencies had long been partners in managing waterfowl populations, but the NAWMP provided clear goals and structure to these partnerships to conserve wetland habitats. It explicitly brought the private sector into these partnerships as well—most prominently Ducks Unlimited (DU).

Serving as a catalyst, DU worked with government agencies to successfully establish public policy, and it solicited the voluntary, but very active involvement of private landowners and other private entities across the continent. The focus of NAWMP partnerships on the protection, restoration, and enhancement of wetlands and waterfowl habitats has demonstrated that a landscape approach to bird conservation can be successful. These efforts have also clearly shown that a habitat focus provides benefits to many species beyond those targeted, and that an ecosystem or landscape approach attracts a broader array of partners. The North American Wetlands Conservation Act has likewise been a critical catalyst for ensuring the viability of these conservation approaches and successfully putting them to work across the national landscape.

The greatest opportunities we have are the expanding partnerships designed to conduct fully integrated bird conservation. State and federal agencies and non-governmental organizations have been working together over the last decade to plan and implement the future of bird conservation with an eye toward integrating their efforts. Grassroots support for addressing the needs of all wildlife is growing, as evidenced by the public support that Partners in Flight and other bird initiatives are experiencing, and by the breadth of the Teaming With Wildlife coalition. This support will continue to increase dramatically.

It is apparent from examples such as the bald eagle and waterfowl that, once brought to the Nation's attention, support for bird conservation is broad and deep. The message is clear: birds are important to the people of the United States and their populations should not be allowed to decline further; but rather should be restored and maintained. The stage is set to move beyond conservation targeted on a few high-profile species or even a group of species and their habitats. Clearly, we are on the threshold of a new era of comprehensive, integrated bird conservation—and we must seize this opportunity.

PRINCIPLES

The NABCI-US will be guided by principles that establish an operational framework and sideboards within which this initiative and its partners will conduct integrated bird conservation in the United States and beyond. These principles address the fundamental components of the NABCI-US goal *to deliver the full spectrum of bird conservation through regionally based, biologically driven, landscape-oriented partnerships.*

"Deliver the full spectrum of bird conservation..."

♦ **There are federal legislative and treaty obligations, as well as state mandates, for the conservation and management of birds.**

♦ **The NABCI-US will respect the identity and autonomy of all individual bird initiatives (e.g., North American Waterfowl Management Plan, Partners in Flight, U.S. Shorebird Conservation Plan, North American Colonial Waterbird Conservation Plan).**

- **Financial resources necessary for comprehensive bird conservation in the United States can be marshaled more effectively by a broad, robust coalition of bird interests than by the individual efforts of separate initiatives.**

- **Financial resources marshaled for bird conservation can be used more effectively when management needs and actions (1) address the needs of birds at the most crucial points in their life cycles and, (2) are integrated across landscapes providing the greatest benefit for the broadest array of species.**

Migratory bird treaties with Canada and Mexico have served as long-standing, enduring international conservation agreements. The treaties and their implementing acts grant ultimate responsibility for safeguarding and managing migratory birds in the United States to the Federal government. However, state wildlife conservation agencies have long been partners in this effort, exercising a shared responsibility for the management of these species. Conversely, authority for resident bird species remains with the states, although the Federal government in various ways has been a partner in their conservation. In addition, both migratory and resident bird species and their habitats are the focus of numerous private organizations representing millions of members. Also, private landowners, through individual action and voluntary, incentive-based conservation programs, have contributed significantly to bird conservation.

Not long ago, "migratory bird conservation" was synonymous with waterfowl and migratory game bird management. Due to the phenomenal growth of outdoor recreation involving non-game birds and the documentation of long-term declines of many of these species, interest among the public, scientists, and managers has increased dramatically. The concern generated by this interest is reflected in the growing number of individual initiatives and organizations with a central bird conservation mission. Understanding that federal and state wildlife agencies are mandated to conserve *all* birds, bird conservation demands that attention be placed on the full array of species throughout the future.

" ...through regionally based, ... "

- **The NABCI-US will promote comprehensive bird conservation based on similarities within geographic regions regarding habitat types, ecosystem components, management issues, and successful conservation approaches.**

- **A common ecological framework is essential to efficient planning, implementation, and evaluation processes for delivering the full spectrum of bird conservation.**

- **The organization of regional partnerships to deliver bird conservation will be based on a sound ecological framework and practical administrative and economic considerations defined by partners.**

Regionally based partnerships are essential for the effective delivery of integrated bird conservation. Various groups of birds often share habitats and conservation challenges.

Similarities in land-use patterns and natural ecosystems exist within identifiable geographic regions of the United States, providing a logical framework for bird conservation. In addition, the people, communities, and organizations within regions can work together more readily in partnerships because of common concerns and opportunities. These similarities provide tremendous opportunities to organize partnerships to deliver management within geographically identified bird conservation regions.

" … biologically driven, … "

♦ **The NABCI-US will be based on the best available scientific information.**

♦ **An adaptive approach to bird conservation is necessary to build our knowledge in concert with our management actions.**

♦ **Effective conservation of bird populations and habitats depends on an understanding of the responses of populations to habitat alterations and management actions, and is driven by linkages between population and habitat objectives.**

Waterfowl have been the focus of research for more than 50 years, yet significant deficiencies in knowledge still exist. Major information gaps likewise prevail regarding the population biology and management of many other bird species. Monitoring bird populations is a necessary first step in focusing conservation efforts. In addition, scientific information relating habitat alteration and management actions to changes in bird populations is essential for measuring effectiveness and refining management actions. The NABCI-US must be science-based to most effectively use the financial resources dedicated to bird conservation.

" … landscape-oriented … "

♦ **Bird populations respond to landscape-level conditions, as well as changes in those conditions, throughout their population ranges.**

♦ **Bird conservation objectives should be incorporated into existing natural resource practices and programs as much as possible.**

♦ **The NABCI-US will promote sustainable land-use and management practices most compatible with bird conservation.**

♦ **Bird conservation can help provide for the conservation of other wildlife groups and natural resources from a broader perspective.**

Birds exist within landscapes that serve a variety of purposes. Incorporating "greenspace" into urban and suburban development now will certainly play a role in the future of bird conservation. Agricultural practices and Federal farm policies have important, direct effects on bird conservation efforts because many landscapes are predominantly agricultural. Management of private and public forests, grasslands, and wetlands affects landscapes at regional scales. Clearly, the broad habitat implications of responsible bird conservation both within and outside the United States can directly benefit many other groups of wildlife sharing the same landscapes. Furthermore, a landscape approach allows bird conservation to be successfully integrated into sustainable land-use patterns, helping to meet the current and future needs of society.

" ... partnerships. "

♦ **Effective bird conservation depends on the cooperation of independent agencies and organizations at international, national, regional, state, and local geographic scales.**

♦ **The NABCI-US will build and strengthen the diverse linkages among public agencies, private organizations, landowners, and individuals at all geographic levels of conservation delivery.**

♦ **Bird conservation efforts will include a broad array of options, emphasizing policies that promote voluntary stewardship approaches and strategies that are highly leveraged to maximize the use of scarce resources.**

♦ **Bird conservation partners will identify and resolve potential conflicts among priority bird conservation needs within a geographic area.**

♦ **Through training and education-based partnerships, the NABCI-US will broaden public awareness about the importance and relevance of bird conservation to society.**

The single most important component of bird conservation is partnerships. In any cooperative venture, each partner—federal, state, tribal, non-governmental, or individual—must come to the table voluntarily and be willing to share its resources to achieve common goals. Successful partnerships contain partners that understand and respect each other's independent missions. They also find common ground and follow management actions that result in the most efficient use of resources. Because of legislative mandates, the Federal government must take the lead in providing the basic resources required for integrated bird conservation across state and national boundaries; but it must also seek a broad partnership among the states, non-governmental organizations, and private citizens. Successful conservation partnership models like the North American Waterfowl Management Plan and the North American Wetlands Conservation Act show the way, providing a working foundation upon which to build broader, deeper partnerships on behalf of bird conservation in the United States and beyond.

HISTORY AND STATUS OF BIRD CONSERVATION INITIATIVES
In the United States

Background

The surge of interest in birds has resulted in several unprecedented bird conservation initiatives such as the North American Waterfowl Management Plan, Partners in Flight, the U.S. Shorebird Conservation Plan, and the North American Colonial Waterbird Conservation Plan. The North American Bird Conservation Initiative (NABCI) as a whole is facilitating linkages among these individual initiatives, both within and among the United States, Mexico, and Canada. Since no two countries are alike, each one decides for itself how best to advance the common principles of NABCI within its borders. The following overview of the evolution of bird conservation in the United States provides an important context for understanding the trajectory of bird conservation efforts today.

Bird conservation in the United States is rooted in history, public attitudes, and landscape protection. Designation of the first National Wildlife Refuge (NWR) in 1903—an 8-acre island off the coast of Florida—marked an important point in the history of bird conservation. Pelican Island NWR was established to protect pelicans and other colonial nesting birds from the excessive millinery trade. By this time, it had become clear that unregulated market hunting, or the harvest of wildlife for profit, was a significant threat to birds. State and Federal agencies responded with laws regulating hunting and initiated biological studies to learn more about bird population dynamics. Internationally, the 1916 and 1936 Migratory Bird Conventions with Canada and Mexico, respectively, and the 1918 Migratory Bird Treaty Act (MBTA) regulated the take of migratory birds in North America. They also made migratory bird protection a responsibility of the federal governments. A strong tradition of international cooperation in waterfowl population surveys and harvest management followed.

As human use of the continent intensified, so did the loss of and adverse impacts on bird habitats. In response, federal and state governments accelerated acquisition and management of the most critical habitats. Waterfowl were a major focus, particularly for the NWR system. State land acquisition often revolved around game species because its primary source of funding came from hunters and anglers. Later, endangered species and other migratory birds gained more prominence in the setting of conservation priorities on public lands. More recent habitat-focused international agreements, such as the 1971 Ramsar Convention on Wetlands of International Importance, have provided a framework for national action and international cooperation for the conservation of wetlands and their resources.

Throughout the 20th century, the role of citizens and non-governmental organizations has been pivotal in moving the Nation's bird conservation agenda forward. The three major bird-focused crises of the last 100 years include the "plume crisis" of the first decade, the Dust Bowl Era of the 1920's and 30's, and the post-WWII pesticide crisis. Citizens assertively responded to these events by pushing governmental action and legislative resolutions such as the MBTA, Lacey Act, Federal Duck Stamp Program, NWR system expansion, Pittman-Robertson Act, and Endangered Species Act. They banded together to form organizations such as the National Audubon Society, Ducks Unlimited, National Wildlife Federation, and many others that worked to actively promote these bird conservation measures—and still aggressively do so today. The positive actions of the past were a direct result of the grassroots actions of citizens and non-governmental organizations.

Now at the start of the 21st century, with populations of many birds still declining, even more concerted actions and innovative solutions are needed to achieve our bird conservation goals. The major individual bird conservation initiatives in the United States, and the comprehensive, international focus of NABCI, arose out of a recognition that effective bird conservation requires:

- *a strong scientific understanding of birds, their habitats, and population phenomena;*
- *conservation and management at local, landscape, continental, and hemispheric scales; and*
- *the involvement of all elements of human society that affect and are affected by changes in bird populations.*

Flyway Council System

The flyway council system pioneered the first formalized, interagency, cooperative partnership on behalf of migratory bird management in North America. This system enabled states, the Federal government, and several non-governmental organizations to develop the processes and working relationships needed for co-managing the migratory bird resource. In so doing, this system laid the critical foundation for the creation of future migratory bird initiatives such as the North American Waterfowl Management Plan.

In 1947, the U.S. Fish and Wildlife Service designated four "flyways" as bio-administrative units within which to manage waterfowl populations. States quickly recognized the flyway system as an opportunity for cooperative management of waterfowl and as a forum for promoting states' interests in the regulatory process. Resolution Number 10 was passed in 1951 by the International Association of Game, Fish, and Conservation Commissioners (now the International Association of Fish and Wildlife Agencies [IAFWA]), and in 1952, councils were formed for the Pacific, Central, Mississippi, and Atlantic Flyways. A primary purpose of the council system was to establish hunting regulations based on waterfowl biology and distribution, as well as to acknowledge different hunting interests and conditions across the country. The National Waterfowl Council, composed of a representative from each flyway council, was formed in 1953 to further each council's objectives.

Today, the councils serve as the primary administrative vehicles for provinces, states, and federal agencies to cooperatively manage waterfowl populations. Although the original role of the councils focused heavily on hunting regulations, they soon began to address broader waterfowl-related issues. Now, the councils work to better understand and improve conditions for waterfowl productivity, distribution, harvest, and habitat management.

Technical advisory committees have been established within each flyway to better address issues such as these.

In 1995, the IAFWA conducted a Flyway System Review and recommended that the management of all migratory birds be coordinated through the flyway councils. For example, councils may consider establishing new technical committees, in addition to waterfowl and webless game bird committees, to address issues associated with other bird populations in the flyways. Currently, coot, gallinule, rail, and snipe seasons are set in reference to flyways. Also, mourning dove and woodcock management units have been modeled after the flyway concept.

The North American Waterfowl Management Plan

Migratory bird conservation entered a new phase when the United States and Canada signed the North American Waterfowl Management Plan (Plan) in 1986, followed by Mexico in 1994. This international agreement challenged conservationists in North America to restore waterfowl populations to levels recorded in the 1970's. Most importantly, it directed that this be accomplished by creating sustainable landscapes for waterfowl using unprecedented partnerships among the federal, state, and private sectors. Many factors contributed to the success of the Plan, but a focused and organized constituency was particularly key. This constituency facilitated the passage of the 1989 North American Wetlands Conservation Act—the primary funding tool for habitat conservation under the Plan.

Over the last decade, Plan partners have created a highly successful model for effective conservation: regional partnerships called "joint ventures" that deliver biologically based habitat conservation on landscapes important to waterfowl. Each of the 11 U.S. habitat joint ventures is guided by an implementation plan laying out measurable population targets and corresponding habitat objectives. Population targets are linked to continental population goals expressed in the Plan.

More than 4.9 million acres of wetlands and associated upland habitats have been conserved in the United States under the Plan, at an investment of over $1.5 billion. These efforts, and those of other wildlife and agricultural conservation policies and programs, have contributed significantly to the rebound of most waterfowl species. However, the work of waterfowl conservation is not done. Increased demands on natural resources from a growing human population and the cyclic return to below-average water conditions in breeding areas will depress waterfowl populations again in the future. Furthermore, the monitoring of several species, including sea ducks, is still not sufficient to adequately assess their status, but they are suspected to be declining.

Plan partners are faced with the challenge of carrying waterfowl conservation's tremendous momentum into the next century. Their conservation efforts must be woven into the rapidly changing and more complex social, economic, and environmental fabric of the 21st century.

Trends point to increased urbanization, a declining proportion of hunters, increasing numbers of birdwatchers, increasing demands for grain, and global climate change. Plan partners are working to respond to the management implications of these trends and also strengthen the biological foundation of waterfowl conservation.

Partners In Flight

Partners In Flight (PIF) is a consortium of public and private organizations and individuals working to conserve landbirds throughout the Western Hemisphere. Its guiding principles are to restore populations of the most imperiled species and to prevent other birds from becoming endangered—"keeping common birds common." Because landbirds are spread diffusely across every habitat type on the continent, PIF may face the most complex challenges among the bird initiatives. Populations of landbirds that can adapt to the dominating presence of humans are thriving, while many less adaptable species are declining. Identifying precise causes of decline is difficult, particularly for migratory species that depend on several habitat types during an annual cycle. Problems facing landbirds often stem from land use driven by societal needs for food, fiber, and living space. Thus, landbird conservation requires a commitment to research and monitoring, and an even more fundamental commitment to developing alliances with people who own, manage, and make decisions about land. Strengthening the link between science and bird conservation lies at the core of the PIF philosophy.

Partners anticipate completing the Regional Bird Conservation Plans for landbirds in the continental United States by the end of 2000. These plans are based upon species prioritization, resulting in a list of landbirds requiring conservation attention in each region, grouped according to shared habitats. Conditions of priority habitats are then assessed and management recommendations are directed thereafter at habitats, not at individual bird species. The plans strive to present scientifically credible, yet realistic population and habitat objectives, considering current ecological conditions and social and economic realities. With these regional plans, PIF is contributing significantly to more strategic, comprehensive, and effective bird conservation.

Over the past decade, PIF's network of thousands of partners has been involved in a diversity of proactive conservation activities including research and monitoring, habitat management and restoration, technical assistance to federal agencies and other landowners, policy development and advocacy, and outreach and education. Partners have worked at all geographic levels and throughout the Western Hemisphere. However, to be most effective, its activities need to be part of a larger, integrated strategy for delivering bird conservation at all spatial scales.

United States Shorebird Conservation Plan

Shorebirds are among the most amazing migratory birds, generally traveling the longest distances and being on the move the greatest amount of time each year. They seem to "follow the sun," tracking bursts of food resources as they become available, pausing briefly to breed at the northern end of their route before heading south again. Many species concentrate at a series of critical stop-over sites stretching from the Arctic Ocean to the tip of South America. Their natural history is so distinctive that novel conservation actions are needed.

Most shorebirds depend on wetlands for all or much of their life cycles. Habitat loss and various types of degradation, such as human disturbance, pollution, food depletion, and increasing threats from predators, are the main pressures affecting shorebird population declines. Without remedial conservation efforts, these pressures can be expected to increase in the future. Focused conservation actions and integrated management practices are needed to prevent additional shorebird species from becoming threatened or endangered.

The Western Hemisphere Shorebird Reserve Network was founded in 1986 to identify and encourage protection of the most important stop-over and wintering sites in North and South America. This and other conservation efforts in the United States and abroad (e.g., the East Asian Australasian Shorebird Reserve Network) have been very successful at protecting some of the most critical sites and at raising awareness of the special requirements of shorebirds. However, these efforts have been insufficient to secure stable or increasing populations of many species. Ongoing conservation challenges have highlighted the need for comprehensive planning to address critical aspects of shorebird life history.

The U.S. Shorebird Conservation Plan (USSCP) was initiated in 1996 to address this need. The USSCP is a partnership effort designed to ensure that populations of all shorebird species are protected or restored to a healthy condition. This shorebird plan, completed in April 2000, lays out conservation goals for 11 shorebird management regions of the United States and identifies critical habitat conservation and key research needs. It also proposes education and outreach programs to increase awareness about shorebirds and their unique needs.

Fortunately, many shorebird conservation needs are compatible with those of waterfowl. The natural synergy developing between the USSCP and the North American Waterfowl Management Plan is beneficial for both groups of species. Because many shorebirds use upland habitats for nesting or foraging, USSCP objectives are also being aligned with those being developed by Partners in Flight—further contributing to the integration of bird conservation needs.

North American Colonial Waterbird Conservation Plan

This newest bird conservation initiative addresses the needs of colonial waterbirds, which includes a broad array of bird species such as herons and egrets, gulls and terns, and many seabirds. As with waterfowl and shorebirds, protection or restoration of aquatic and wetland habitat is needed for many waterbird species. Still others forage along shorelines and in the open ocean, where problems such as pollution and conflicts with recreation and fisheries must be addressed. Some species such as the double-crested cormorant are overabundant, posing unique challenges to population management. The conservation needs of colonial waterbirds must be addressed on a large geographic scale due to their wide distribution, with some breeding in the United States and Canada and wintering as far south as Mexico or the Caribbean. Maintaining North American populations at appropriate levels, therefore, depends on planning, inventory, monitoring, and management actions on an international and continental scale.

The weak link in the life cycle of all of these birds is their propensity to nest in colonies. Loss of a colony can mean loss of a local population or, in a few cases, extinction of a species. While colonies are sensitive to a wide range of human disturbances, they are particularly susceptible to new or imbalanced predator populations (e.g., rats and cats on nesting islands, and burgeoning gull populations along coastlines).

The North American Colonial Waterbird Conservation Plan (NACWCP) began in 1998 and followed the lead of other successful plans by relying on voluntary partnerships, strong science, and the development of explicit objectives. Components of this plan focus on research and information needs, monitoring, management, and education and outreach. The NACWCP will also coordinate with other bird conservation initiatives to identify regional conservation goals and key habitats, delineate critical research needs, and develop public outreach materials and training programs. The plan's international strategy will be completed by December 2000, and its accompanying regional plans will be available in 2001.

North American Bird Conservation Initiative

The individual bird conservation initiatives have come to recognize their common bond of shared migratory bird habitats. The leaders of each initiative understand that there is not only common ground in the biological landscape, but also significant overlap in institutional frameworks on which the foundation for delivering comprehensive, coordinated migratory bird conservation can be based. However, prior to 1998, no effective mechanism for coordination existed. And although the major current initiatives deal with most birds, some groups such as rails and other non-colonial waterbirds are not included. Geographically, the North American Waterfowl Management Plan covers the United States, Canada, and Mexico, and the North American Colonial Waterbird Plan addresses all of North and Central America and the Caribbean. Partners in Flight's Bird Conservation Plans and the U.S. Shorebird Conservation Plan include only the United States.

In 1998, the Commission for Environmental Cooperation stimulated increased international cooperation. Participants from Canada, the United States, and Mexico brought into existence the North American Bird Conservation Initiative (NABCI). NABCI does not limit the autonomy or independence of any of its participants, but rather seeks to increase the effectiveness of the separate initiatives by integrating conservation objectives and project implementation. NABCI is also working to increase the resources available for bird conservation. In short, NABCI is a tool to help "take bird conservation to the next level." Any success in achieving that goal will be a reflection of the level of desire and commitment of the individual bird conservation initiatives and their partners to work together *to deliver the full spectrum of bird conservation through regionally based, biologically driven, landscape-oriented partnerships.*

CONSERVATION APPROACH

The success of NABCI will ultimately depend upon acceptance and use of a conservation approach that is grounded in sound science and landscape-level, partner-driven delivery. Fortunately, this approach is increasingly being adopted by the individual initiatives.

• **Establishing and Refining a Science Foundation**

The role of science in bird conservation

Successful conservation must be based on sound science, a precept reflected in the phrase "biologically-driven". To achieve the goal of integrated bird conservation, there must be a solid underlying foundation of scientific knowledge about birds and the threats they face. This scientific foundation allows goals to be applied to specific conservation projects that manage birds and their habitats. Science provides the information needed to effectively identify and address critical conservation needs. Effective conservation requires an understanding of the threats birds face, and the critical life history stages and geographic locations at which populations are limited. Unfortunately, this understanding is insufficient or altogether lacking for most birds.

Fundamental scientific information must be developed to guide the refinement of bird conservation priorities, support the design and development of critical conservation projects, and help measure the effectiveness of our actions in meeting our goals. There must be a commitment to this scientific process, even as we must also continue making management decisions without complete information.

Integrated Planning, Implementation, and Evaluation

Effective conservation requires a dynamic process of (1) strategic planning, (2) implementation of management actions, and (3) evaluation of effectiveness. This process of "adaptive resource management" allows managers and scientists to proceed with critical conservation actions in the face of scientific uncertainty. When properly applied, the process permits us to deliver management actions while simultaneously allowing us to learn from and refine our understanding of the effectiveness of those actions.

Planning develops the population and habitat objectives for specific groups of birds. Scientists and managers most familiar with each bird group, particularly its life history needs and limiting factors, should initiate planning. Effective planning also requires consideration of many non-biological factors, such as existing land use, public attitudes, and budget constraints. Therefore, involvement of top management, the public, and decision-makers is crucial.

Implementation delivers the specific conservation projects or other management actions necessary to protect and conserve bird populations. Implementation is most effectively carried out in an integrated fashion, combining the overlapping habitat and management needs of each bird group as part of an overall landscape-level strategy. Integration of bird conservation activities is one of the core principles of NABCI. Implementation requires the participation of the widest possible range of public and private partners. NABCI can benefit even more broadly from working with partners whose primary agendas may not focus on birds, but who still share significant conservation objectives.

Evaluation measures how effectively conservation actions and strategies have achieved overall conservation goals. Although it requires sound scientific information and is critical to ensuring that conservation goals are being achieved, evaluation is not an end in itself. Evaluation activities include analysis of changes in bird populations and assessments of habitat quality and availability. They also encompass targeted studies where critical information is lacking for determining future priorities, and assessments of specific conservation programs. Effective evaluation should increase our understanding of the factors limiting bird populations and how best to address them, thereby contributing to an iterative process of revising the conservation strategies and goals developed during the planning phase.

- **Toward Landscape-Level Conservation**

Managing the conservation of the more than 700 bird species that occur in this country is not practical on a species-by-species basis. Each species may use many different habitats during the year and each habitat type often has unique management challenges. However, at the scale of landscapes, the needs of many different bird species overlap to some degree. Therefore, by combining management needs for species that use the same types of habitat, the needs of a variety of birds can be addressed simultaneously—increasing the efficiency and effectiveness of specific management actions and reducing costs.

By also applying this same approach to the needs of other wildlife species, agriculture, and development, planners can define the nature of future landscapes. All of society's interests, including such needs as flood control, public health, and bird conservation, must coexist on our landscapes. A central goal of NABCI is to help build the partnerships that will achieve truly integrated conservation, and design and promote sustainable environments to help meet the needs and desires of future generations.

- **Forging Broad Partnerships for Bird Conservation**

All conservation ultimately is local. The public and private organizations in each part of the United States and other countries are most knowledgeable about local conditions, needs, and opportunities. They are also most empowered by successful conservation activities in their areas. NABCI adheres to the vision of regionally based partnerships that build on local knowledge and enthusiasm to promote conservation activities for all groups of birds.

Joint ventures, formed to implement the North American Waterfowl Management Plan, provide the most effective model that exists today for public-private conservation partnerships. They have actively involved federal, state, and local governments and a wide range of non-governmental conservation organizations in effective partnerships to generate "on-the-ground" conservation. All joint ventures share the common characteristic of being dynamic, self-directed partnerships that deliver science-based habitat conservation in a distinct geographic area, consistent with national and international bird conservation plans. The existing joint ventures that have already taken steps to embrace the goal of integrated bird conservation provide the first examples of the application of the NABCI vision. In areas without existing partnerships, additional joint ventures will be created to facilitate integrated bird conservation.

THE BIRD CONSERVATION LANDSCAPE
Bird Conservation Regions

Effective integrated bird conservation requires the maintenance or restoration of landscapes in which the quantity, quality, and diversity of suitable habitats meet the needs of all species. Ecology-based landscape units enable efficient conservation because they encompass similar bird communities, similar habitats, and similar land-use and resource issues. Conservation partnerships rooted in this context are not new. At their inception, joint ventures were delineated within ecologically based focus areas of special significance to waterfowl.

Effective conservation delivery requires linking population responses to habitat changes at multiple spatial scales—from the local scale of individual habitat management projects, to continental scales at which national and international program planning and evaluation occur. Consequently, issues of scale have been prominent in NABCI efforts to develop a framework of ecologically based Bird Conservation Regions (BCRs) encompassing North America. It was recognized that BCRs should accommodate varying spatial scales in biological planning and evaluation, and should be flexible enough to allow for the use of multiple scale-specific approaches to on-the-ground management. Furthermore, any ecological framework must respect political boundaries while facilitating innovative bird conservation within states and provinces and among broader partnerships.

NABCI has adopted a four-level hierarchical framework of nested ecological units as the fundamental geographic basis from which to deliver integrated bird conservation in North America. From the most general to the most specific levels, these eco-regions encompass areas that are progressively more similar in their biotic (plant communities and wildlife) and abiotic (soils, drainage patterns, temperature, and annual precipitation) characteristics. Eco-regions at multiple scales may then be combined or partitioned in various combinations to best reflect both the distribution and needs of birds, while preserving the integrity of the ecologically based framework. This eco-region approach will facilitate coordination among natural resource managers working at different spatial scales or in different geographic regions because eco-region building blocks provide common ground.

The purpose of BCRs is to:

- ◆ systematically and scientifically apportion the United States and North America into conservation units;
- ◆ facilitate a regional approach to bird conservation;
- ◆ facilitate communication among bird conservation initiatives; and
- ◆ promote new or expanded partnerships.

BCRs are proposed as a single application of the scale-flexible, hierarchical, ecological framework adopted for integrated bird conservation; not as static or rigid regional units. BCRs may be partitioned into smaller ecological units when finer-scale conservation planning, implementation, and evaluation are necessary. Conversely, BCRs may be aggregated to facilitate conservation partnerships throughout the annual range of a group of species, much as the Flyway approach to partnering has been applied in waterfowl management. Finally, BCRs will also facilitate international cooperation because these areas of relatively homogeneous habitats and bird communities traverse national borders. The fundamental principle is that effective, integrated bird conservation can best take place when executed within an ecologically based, geographical context.

A map of North American BCRs and an accompanying descriptive booklet are provided in the NABCI outreach document, *North American Bird Conservation Initiative: Bringing it all together*. The map reflects our current understanding of species distribution, life history requirements, and conservation challenges, while the booklet offers a brief description of each region.

ADMINISTRATION

The responsibility for leadership in fulfilling the vision of NABCI in the United States rests with the U.S. NABCI Committee. This Committee will initially be composed of 11 individuals, each representing an entity critical to the success of bird conservation:

- Director (or designee), U.S. Fish and Wildlife Service, Co-Chair;
- President (or designee), International Association of Fish and Wildlife Agencies, Co-Chair;
- representative of the North American Waterfowl Management Plan;
- representative of Partners in Flight;
- representative of the U.S. Shorebird Conservation Plan;
- representative of the North American Colonial Waterbird Conservation Plan;
- representative of Ducks Unlimited;
- representative of the Wildlife Management Institute;
- representative of the National Flyway Council;
- Chair of the Non-Governmental Organization Subcommittee; and
- Co-chair of the Federal Agency Subcommittee.

The U.S. NABCI Committee will initially have three permanent subcommittees: a Federal Agency Subcommittee, a Non-Governmental Organization Subcommittee, and a Monitoring Subcommittee. The roles, responsibilities, and operating procedures of the U.S. NABCI Committee and its subcommittees are defined in its charter, but will primarily serve three functions:

1. To represent the United States internationally within the North American Bird Conservation Initiative, appointing three U.S. representatives to the Tri-national NABCI Steering Committee;

2. To provide a forum for interaction among U.S. bird conservation initiatives, and facilitate collaboration and communication among partnerships delivering integrated bird conservation; and,

3. To endeavor to increase the resources available for the conservation of U.S. birds wherever they may occur throughout their life cycles.

The Committee will be staffed by a National Coordinator. However, additional ad-hoc staff support will most likely be necessary to address the full range of Committee functions and tasks. The Committee will address the composition and structure of this staff support on an as-needed basis.

Additional copies of this document may be obtained from:

U.S. Fish and Wildlife Service
Division of North American Waterfowl and Wetlands
4401 N. Fairfax Drive, Suite 110
Arlington, VA 22203
(703) 358-1784

Illustrations by Bob Hines, U.S. Fish and Wildlife Service

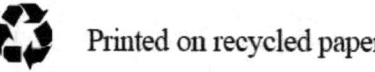